I0505488

# How to Select Your Internet Marketing Niche

## A Fundamental Decision

Book 2 in the Internet Marketing FAST Series

# Copyright and Enquiries

Copyright © 2019-2024 by Phillip J. Lancaster

All rights reserved. This book or any portion thereof may not be reproduced or used in any manner whatsoever without the express written permission of the publisher except for the use of brief quotations in a book review.

Comments or enquiries may be left in the *Contact Me* page at:

https://superaffiliatechallenge.com/contact-me/

# Contents

# How to Select Your IM Niche

A Fundamental Decision

# How to Select Your IM Niche

A Fundamental Decision

## Table of Figures

# How to Select Your IM Niche

A Fundamental Decision

## Select a Niche

### Internet Marketing Starts with Selecting a Niche

*Figure 1: Selecting a Niche: It Isn't That Hard*

If you are starting any sort of business, whether it's bricks and mortar or an online business, the first question you have to ask yourself is "What is my business all about?"

In the online world, it's called choosing your niche and, although it's very important, bear in mind that it may be just the first of many online businesses that you are going to own.

# How to Select Your IM Niche

A Fundamental Decision

## What Is a Niche Market?

A niche is the subject matter or theme that your business is going to be all about. Although selecting a niche may sound simple or trivial, it is a decision that you should give careful consideration to. It's the first important decision that you have to make in the long process of developing an online business.

Your niche is what your entire website or blog will be based on, and so should be something that is both appealing to yourself and to the visitors that you want to attract to your site and make sales to.

Ideally, your selected niche should be something that you can put your personal spin on, that you know something about or that you are willing to learn about.

*Figure 2: An Attractive, Specialized Niche*

# How to Select Your IM Niche

A Fundamental Decision

An example of a broad niche would be to build a website based on cameras, whereas a more targeted or narrow niche would be to base your website on Nikon lenses or using drones to create stunning video.

Unlike the bricks and mortar world, it costs very little to start an online business so the chances are that you will eventually own several.

This of course has the advantage that each one only needs to earn a small amount for it to all add up to a decent income. And if just one of them takes off, you can do very well indeed.

But it also means don't hesitate too much.

Avoid "paralyses by analysis" and jump right in, even if it's just for the learning experience.

## The Niche Selection Process

People make millions of searches on the internet each day, covering just about every subject imaginable.

### Does Your Niche Get Search Traffic?

The first things to consider is if there is a reasonable number of people searching for the niche that you have in mind. Does the niche that you're considering get a lot of online searches? Although it is important to have a potential audience for your niche, sometimes a niche can be very profitable with a very small audience, especially if it means lower competition.

Does your chosen niche have a potential audience at all, regardless of how small it might be? A sub-niche (for example, Nikon camera lenses or drone videos rather than photography) can be very profitable with less competition.

# How to Select Your IM Niche

A Fundamental Decision

## Can You Create Content?

The second thing to consider is the fact that you are going to be creating content based on the subject matter that you choose, so how much do you know about your niche? Can you easily write content on the subject that you have chosen or are you going to struggle to come up with new ideas after writing a couple of pages? Is there plenty of research material?

*Figure 3: Struggling to Find Ideas*

Is your niche too narrow or too broad? While a broad niche will give you a lot of scope to come up with lots of sub-niches, selecting a very narrow niche may give you a very small audience. However, with a narrow niche and small audience, you generally will find that your viewers are more targeted.

# How to Select Your IM Niche

A Fundamental Decision

## Is Your Niche Profitable?

And the third thing to consider is can you sell product into that niche and make money from it?

Amazon is your first port of call here.

If there's a lot of niche related product on Amazon, that's a great sign. For two reasons. One, it means other people are making money from it and two, you can become an Amazon affiliate and promote those very same products.

Your next check is a Google search. Search for [niche] affiliate.

For example, here's a search for affiliate programs related to drones.

# How to Select Your IM Niche

A Fundamental Decision

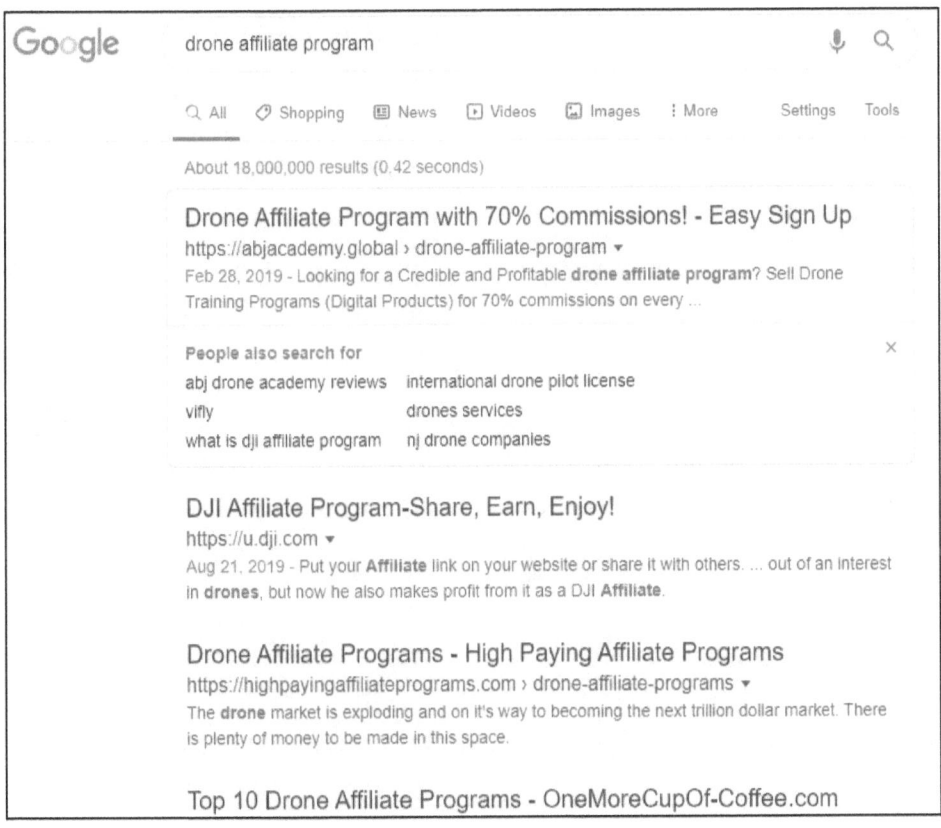

*Figure 4: Search for Drone Affiliate Programs*

There are many pages of drone related products that offer affiliate programs, some with very high commissions.

Most affiliate programs, including Amazon, will require you to submit your website for approval as part of the application process. So you need to have it up and running and looking good first.

What's the best way to finally decide what is best for you?

# How to Select Your IM Niche

A Fundamental Decision

## How to Find a Niche That's Right for You

Over the years, I have built many websites. Some of my sites have been really successful, whilst others have not done so well. But in every mistake that I have ever made, I have always tried to learn from it and correct my mistakes on the next site.

Making a mistake when selecting your niche is really easy to do and sometimes you won't even realize it until you are much further down the line in the content creation stages of building your site.

One of the worst mistakes that you can make when choosing your niche is to go with something simply because you think it's going to make you the most money or to go into something just because you know it's popular and the niche has a large following. Which also means more competition.

It's all very well finding a popular niche, but you need to actually create content and give an opinion based on that subject. Remember that the related sub niches that are associated with the niche that you choose are the subjects that are going to make up the content of your website.

# How to Select Your IM Niche

A Fundamental Decision

*Figure 5: Challenge Visitors with Your Opinion*

Hopefully, you are going to be building that content for a long time, so the last thing that you should choose is something that you know very little about.

Over the years of building websites, I have come to a major conclusion that I hope will help you in selecting the niche for your site.

## Monetize Your Passion

The most important thing, above everything else when selecting your niche is to choose something that you are passionate about. I have seen all kinds of systems and methods online to help find the perfect niche, but they are all pointless if you have no interest in the subject.

Sure, you can go out onto the internet and do research into your chosen subject, but you won't be able to continuously build more content like that if you have no interest in it.

This is the process that I recommend for choosing your business, blog or website's niche. This might sound very simple, but in my opinion this

# How to Select Your IM Niche

A Fundamental Decision

matter does not need to be over complicated, especially if you are new to internet marketing or creating a website.

## Answer These Questions

Ask yourself these questions:

- What are my interests?
- What am I really passionate about?
- Can I write about my chosen subject?
- Does my chosen niche have a following?
- Can I offer an opinion within my niche?
- Do the people within my niche purchase products related to the subject?
- Are there niche products that I could possibly review?
- Is my niche going to be around for a long time?

## Know Your Interests and Expertise

Let's break this down a little. As I have already said, it's essential to have a passion and be interested in your subject matter above everything else. If you are really interested in a subject then you will find it much easier to write about and create the all-important content that your website is going to need.

## Can You Acquire an Audience?

Does your niche have a following? You should be able to find out quite easily by doing a search online to see how many websites are targeting your niche. Don't worry too much about the number of sites that are targeting your niche. Generally speaking, you will find it near impossible to find a niche that has not been covered many times by someone else.

# How to Select Your IM Niche

A Fundamental Decision

*Figure 6: You Must Acquire an Audience*

What makes your site unique is your own spin on things. This is why you should ask "Can I give an opinion within my niche?" It doesn't matter if your opinion is right or wrong. One person's opinion never makes everyone happy.

So long as you are not offensive to anyone or are giving out information that is misleading or potentially harmful, then say what you like! It's your opinions and personality that will make your website or blog unique. Some people will like you for who you are and some won't. That's just how it goes. Don't bother trying to make everyone happy, because it simply won't happen all of the time.

# How to Select Your IM Niche

A Fundamental Decision

## Getting a Return on Investment

How do you intend to make money from your online business? There are lots of ways to do it, but it's also useful to know if there are products that you can promote or review within your niche before you start.

*Figure 7: It All Comes Down to ROI*

Other books in this series will cover affiliate marketing, e-commerce, dropshipping, own product development and the all-important metrics to ensure you have a positive ROI.

## Niche Longevity

Finally ask yourself is your niche going to be around for a long time or is it going to be something that is popular today but gone tomorrow? You need to bear in mind that a popular website does not grow its audience

# How to Select Your IM Niche

overnight. It takes time to build and grow a profitable and successful online business, so you should be prepared to work on your subject for several months to come. While a very new and unique niche may well be very easy to rank for within the search engines, it's not much use if the niche is no longer very popular once you have your blog articles ranked within Google.

## So How Do You Select a Niche?

There are two ways to select a niche for your online business:

1. Choose something that you are knowledgeable, even passionate about. In other words, a familiar subject.
2. Choose something that gets a lot of searches and has a large number of related products. In other words, a popular subject.

### Familiar Subject as Internet Niche: Advantage

The advantage of a familiar subject is that you are going to be writing a lot of content around it and that will be easier if you are already knowledgeable and passionate about it.

The aim of your website is to provide useful and valuable information about your subject to your visitors so that you become an authority in your niche. You can do this by writing articles that address different aspects of your subject (and which also target keywords aimed at getting you ranked in the search engines).

You might also write an e-book on your niche that you give away on your website in exchange for your visitor's name and email address so that you can subsequently send offers to them.

You don't even have to write the book yourself. For a very low price, you can buy PLR (Private Label Rights) to a book that has already been written for your niche. PLR means you can do anything you want with it, including

# How to Select Your IM Niche

making changes to the content, creating a new cover image and claiming authorship.

If you want to make your PLR book unique, just ask ChatGPT to rephrase it, paragraph by paragraph.

You can even get ChatGPT or another AI to write your book for you. It's best to approach this by first asking the AI to create chapter headings and then getting it to write paragraphs for each chapter.

For extra income, you can publish your book on Amazon both as an e-book and a paperback. It's free to do so and can create an extra income stream. I'll explain how to do this in another book in this series.

## Familiar Subject as Internet Niche: Disadvantage

The disadvantage of this approach is that while you may be passionate about a subject, if no one else is, then you won't get much in the way of visitors so all your good work in writing articles will be wasted.

Just because you're passionate about collecting old bottle caps or mapping the far side of the moon doesn't mean that visitors will flock to your specialized website or that you can make an income out of it.

## Popular Subject as Internet Niche: Advantage

By choosing a niche that has a lot of searches and associated products, you increase the chances that, if your business is successful, you can make a lot of money from it.

For example, "weight loss" is one of the most searched for terms on the internet and has a ton of products associated with it, from diet books to treadmills.

So is it a good niche to be in?

# How to Select Your IM Niche

A Fundamental Decision

For a startup business, probably not.

## Popular Subject as Internet Niche: Disadvantage

The disadvantage of a popular subject is, well, its popularity. It means that the competition is intense.

A Google search for "weight loss" will bring up over 1 billion results!

And all of them will have been in business for much longer than you. Every keyword you can think of will already be the subject of other websites.

Your chances of making it to page 1 of Google, Bing or Yahoo through SEO are pretty much zero and if you're not on page 1, you might as well be invisible.

Yes, you can pay for ads, and I'll examine that option in detail further down the track, but for the uninitiated, it's a rapid way to spend money with no return.

## Summary

Choose something that you really want to speak about and that others want to know about. Think in terms of helping others and finding solutions to people's problems. Choose a niche that goes off in various directions and ensure that you are happy to go in those directions too. Select a niche that you can confidently say that you have a real passion for and you won't go far wrong.

But... make sure that it can be profitable as well.

## What to Do?

Clearly, your best bet is to find something that you're knowledgeable about (or at least interested in) that will have a reasonable number of

# How to Select Your IM Niche

related searches but doesn't have an insane amount of competition and has associated products that you can sell.

What we are talking about here is selling products as an affiliate. That is, selling someone else's products that are related to your niche and you earn a commission. This is probably the best model for starting out with a money-making blog.

*Figure 8: Affiliate Marketing*

Other models are advertising on your blog, drop-shipping products bought wholesale (e-commerce) and, of course, the ultimate of developing and selling your own products for 100% of the profit.

I will be covering all of these models as we proceed through this journey. There will be 16 mini-books all together in the Internet Marketing FAST series. 8 have been written so far.

# How to Select Your IM Niche

A Fundamental Decision

## How to Select a (Profitable) Niche

We've covered the considerations involved in selecting a niche.

But you probably want to know exactly HOW to go about it.

Well, it's all about:

# Keyword Research

There, you knew I'd get technical sooner or later, didn't you?

You see, the thing you want to do with your website is to rank highly in the search engines for particular keywords related to your niche.

Which means you need to find keywords (and note that while we call them "words" we actually mean phrases, so that, for example, "exercise routines for seniors" is a "keyword") that have a good number of searches but not so much competition.

But how do we find out?

## Keyword Research Tools

Easy. There are a number of free keyword research tools for you to use. Here are some of them.

## Using the Moz Keyword Explorer

Go to https://moz.com/explorer and enter your keyword (we'll use bike clothing as an example) into the Moz search box.

# How to Select Your IM Niche

A Fundamental Decision

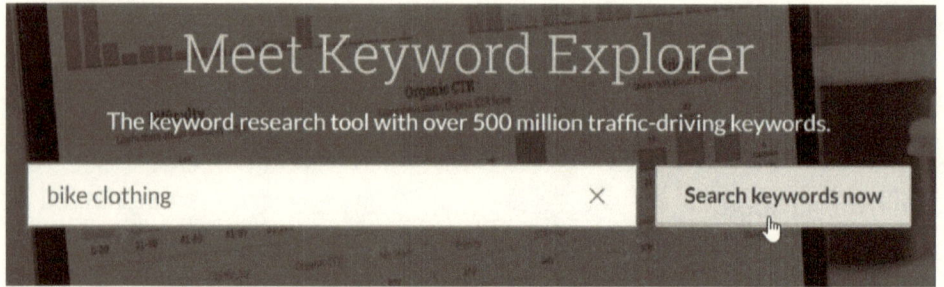

*Figure 9: Search the Moz Keyword Explorer*

You will then be asked to create a Moz account.

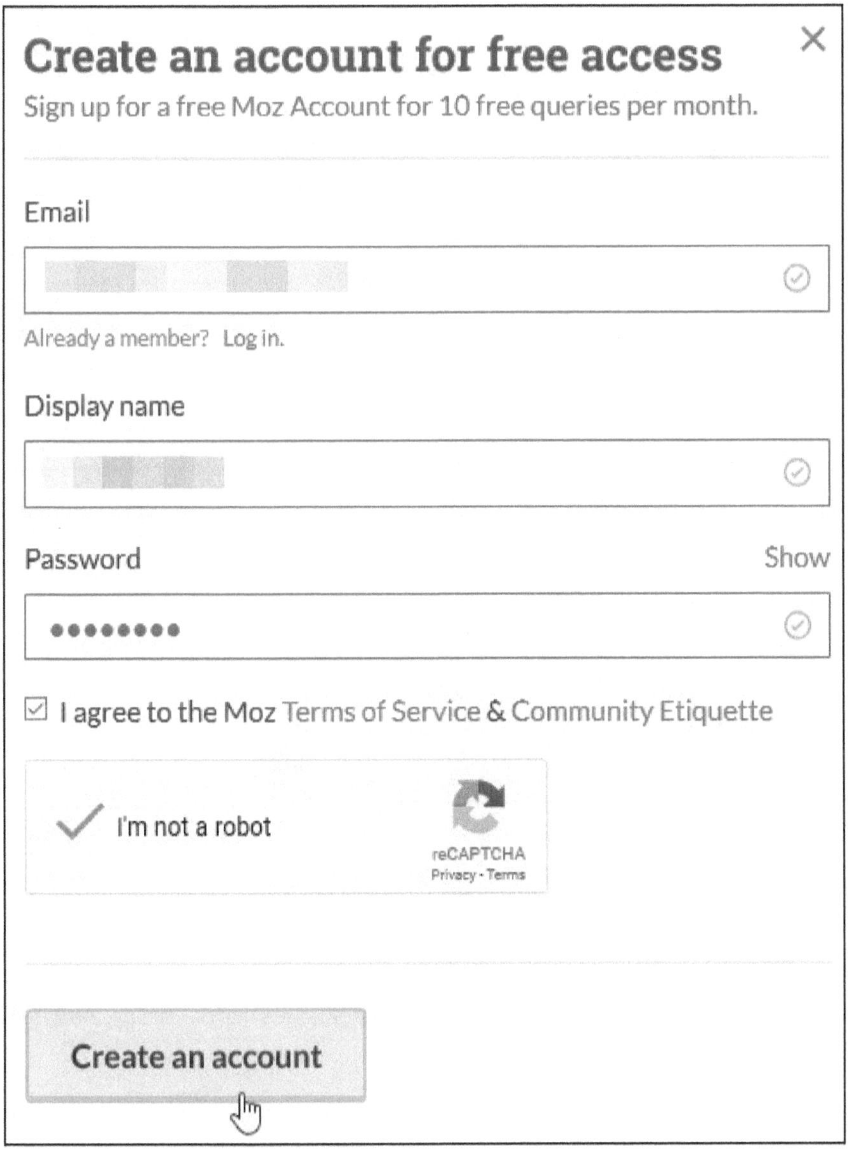

# How to Select Your IM Niche

A Fundamental Decision

## Create an account for free access ✕

Sign up for a free Moz Account for 10 free queries per month.

**Email**

Already a member?  Log in.

**Display name**

**Password**                                                    Show

☑ I agree to the Moz Terms of Service & Community Etiquette

✓ I'm not a robot

reCAPTCHA
Privacy · Terms

**Create an account**

*Figure 10: Create a Moz Account*

# How to Select Your IM Niche

A Fundamental Decision

You're almost there. Moz will send you an email with an activation link. Click the link in the email to activate your account and do your first keyword search.

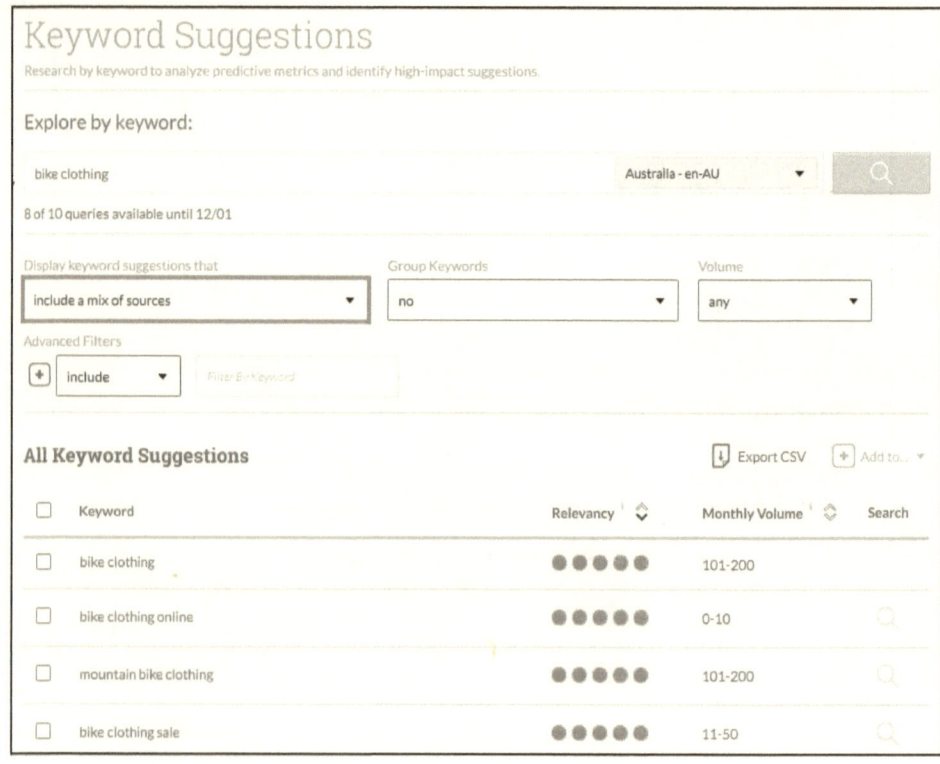

*Figure 11: Moz Keyword Suggestions*

Moz will give you a thousand keyword suggestions, along with their metrics, so it's a very powerful tool.

A free account gives you 10 searches per calendar month. There are other benefits too, which are worth exploring.

# How to Select Your IM Niche

A Fundamental Decision

## The Google Keyword Planner

The Google Keyword Planner is part of the whole "make money for Google through Google Ads" scene but nonetheless can provide useful insights.

Go to https://ads.google.com/home/tools/keyword-planner/ and click on the **Go to Keyword Planner** button.

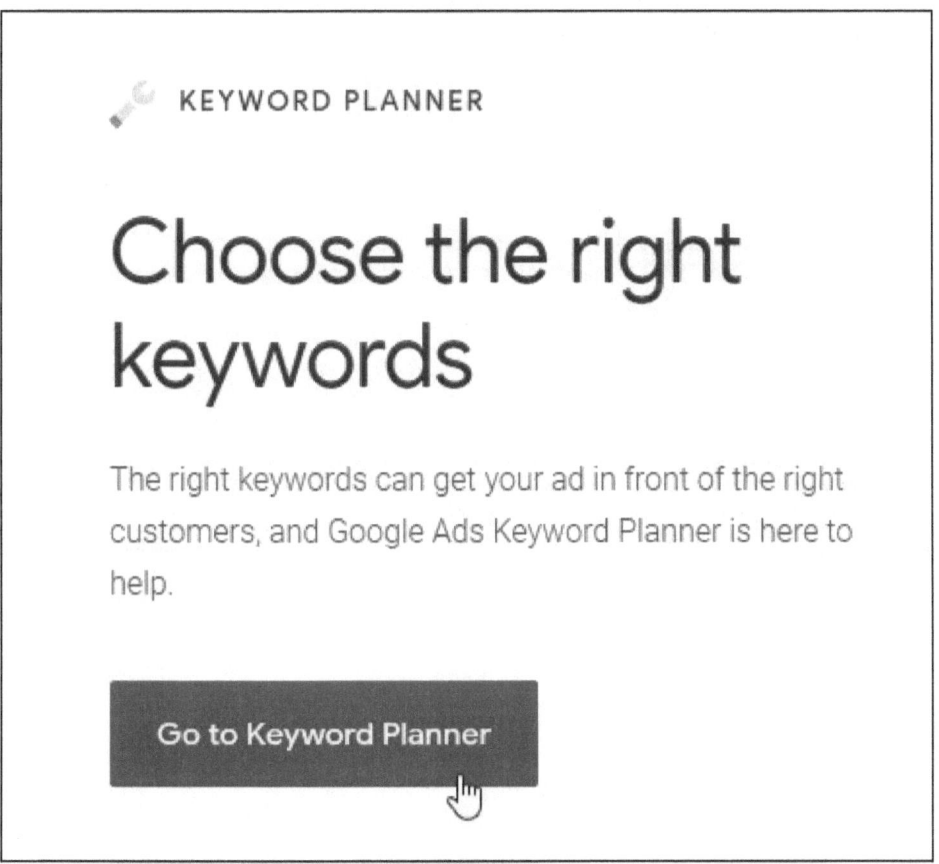

*Figure 12: Click Go to Keyword Planner*

Then click the **Get Started** button.

# How to Select Your IM Niche

A Fundamental Decision

Keyword Planner is a free tool.

But, like most things Google, there's a catch:

In order to use the Google Keyword Planner, you NEED to have a Google Ads account.

If you don't have a Google Ads (previously called AdWords) account already, you can set one up in a few minutes:

Go to https://ads.google.com and click the **Start Now** button.

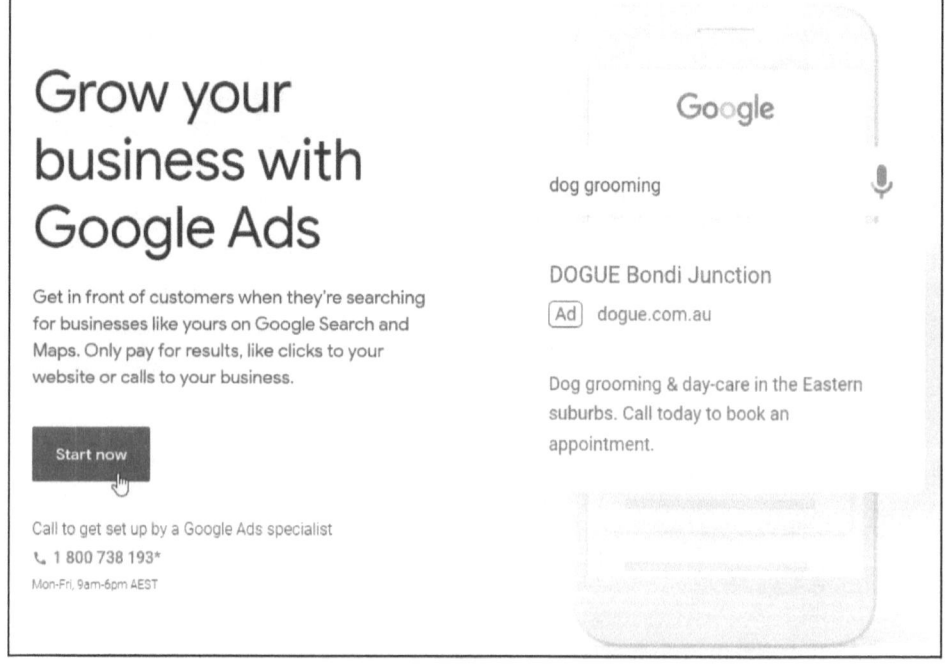

*Figure 13: Apply for a Google Ads Account*

Click on Create Account and follow the process through.

# How to Select Your IM Niche

A Fundamental Decision

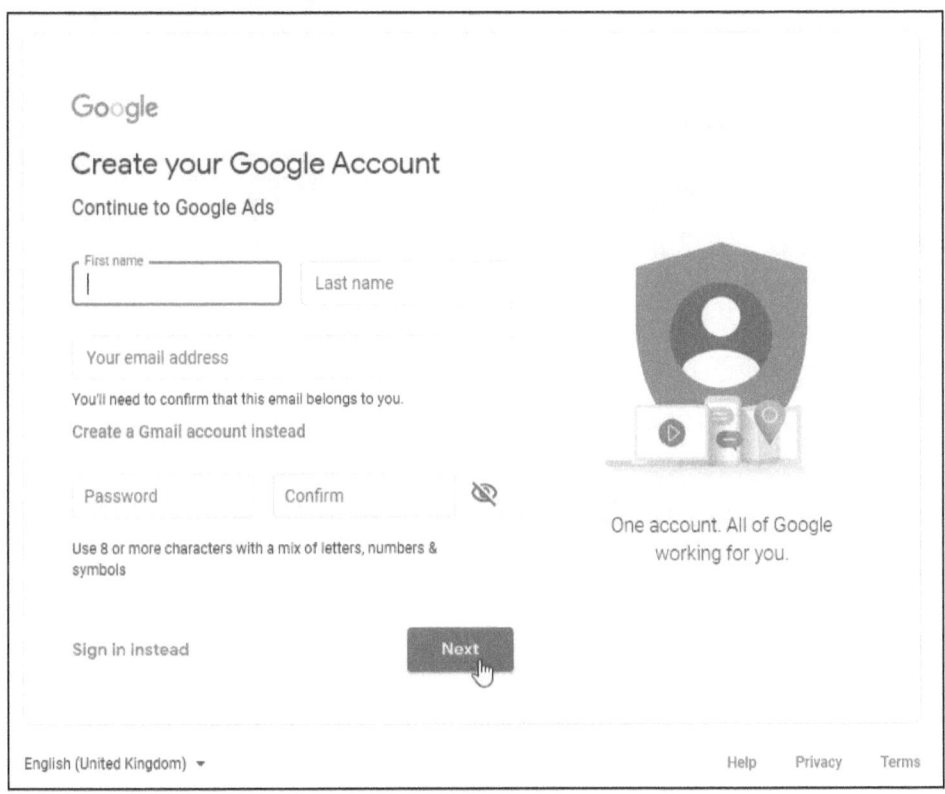

*Figure 14: Start Google Account Creation*

Note that you don't have to run an active campaign to use the Keyword Planner. But you do need to at least set up a Google Ads campaign.

# How to Select Your IM Niche

A Fundamental Decision

*Figure 15: Click on Discover New Keywords*

# How to Select Your IM Niche

A Fundamental Decision

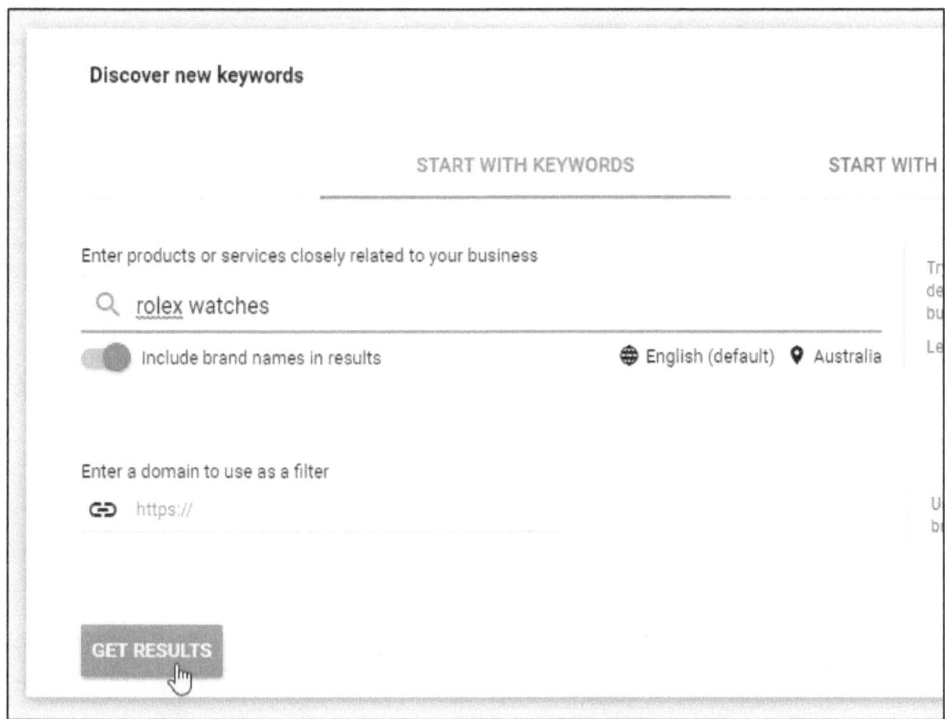

*Figure 16: Enter a Keyword and Click Get Results*

The Google Keyword Planner will return hundreds or even thousands of keyword variations, with extremely valuable insights about each one, including:

- The average number of searches per month for the past 12 months
- The competition level (High, Medium or Low)
- What you would need to bid on a Google Ad to get to the top of the page. This is given as a range, low to high.

# How to Select Your IM Niche

A Fundamental Decision

*Figure 17: Search Results for Rolex Watch Keyword*

You can scroll down to see more results.

You are looking for keyword variations that have reasonably high search volume and low competition.

These will either become the focus of blog posts that link to your monetized landing pages or of ad campaigns.

Weight loss, as part of the health and fitness niche, can be very profitable but also very competitive.

You need to specialize.

Let's use the Google Keyword Planner to look at *weight loss for women*.

# How to Select Your IM Niche

A Fundamental Decision

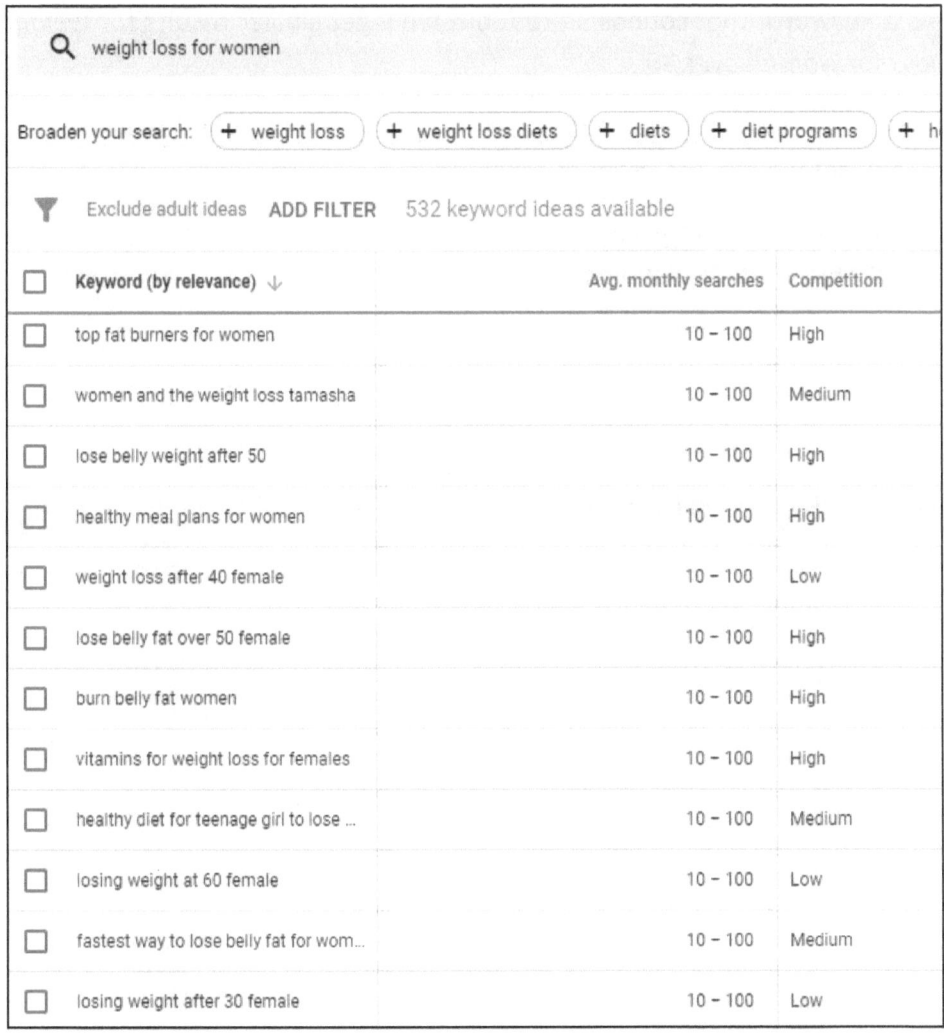

*Figure 18: Results of Weight Loss for Women in Google*

Looking at these results, it appears that there is less competition for specific age groups.

For example, *losing weight after 30 female* is Low.

# How to Select Your IM Niche

A Fundamental Decision

As a keyword, that sounds stilted, but we'll get similar results for *weight loss for women over 30*.

It would be worth writing a blog post targeting this keyword and linking to a relevant weight loss product as an affiliate.

There are many other keywords that could be worth targeting, such as *weight loss diets (for) women over 50*.

## Free Keyword Research Tool

You could also try Ryan Robinson's Free Keyword Research Tool at https://www.ryrob.com/keyword-tool/.

Let's examine some possibilities within the cycling niche.

# How to Select Your IM Niche

A Fundamental Decision

## Free Keyword Research Tool:
### (AI-Powered) SEO Keyword Research & Ideas

**Researching the best keyword ideas for your blog?** This free keyword research tool will help you find blog ideas, identify low competition keywords, find monthly search volume, see the ranking difficulty, and much more! Simply type your keywords below to get started.

EXPLORER    IDEAS                                                                    US US

road bike clothing                                                          SUBMIT

Examples: California Hikes    iPhone Apps    Email Marketing

| KEYWORD | VOLUME | DIFFICULTY |
|---|---|---|
| road bike clothing | 590 | very high |
| casual road bike clothing | 20 | high |
| womens road bike clothing | 50 | very high |
| mens road bike clothing | 50 | very high |

*Figure 19: Keyword Research Road Bike Clothing*

Have a look at road bike clothing above.

The keyword tool tells us that the monthly search volume is 590 (quite low) but that the difficulty is very high, meaning that there's a lot of competition. This is the opposite of what we want.

33

# How to Select Your IM Niche

A Fundamental Decision

This doesn't mean that the niche is bad, just that keyword. Let's refine it a bit further.

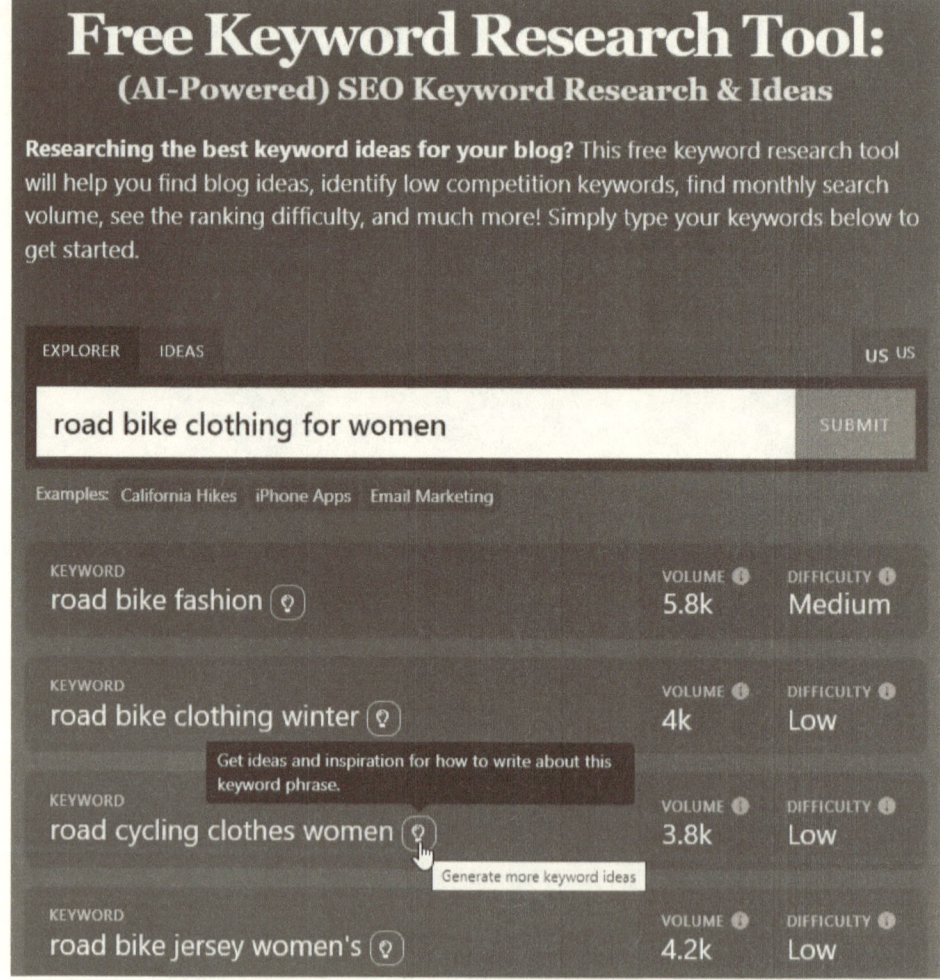

*Figure 20: Road Bike Clothing for Women*

Just by niching down a bit further, by adding the phrase "for women", we've uncovered some excellent ideas.

# How to Select Your IM Niche

A Fundamental Decision

For example, "road cycling clothes (for) women" has 3,800 searches per month with low competition, so this is a keyword you can write an informative article about and direct your readers to relevant affiliate products.

## Niche and Keywords

I hope this has given you some ideas about deciding on the niche for your (first) business.

Start off with something you have an interest in, such as Health and Fitness.

Do some research to determine a good sub-niche, such as Weight Loss for Women.

Search for products that you can promote in that sub-niche.

Use Moz, the Google Keyword Planner and the Free Keyword Research Tool to determine if there are keywords that you can rank on.

# How to Select Your IM Niche

A Fundamental Decision

## The Rest of the Books

Here are all the books in my Internet Marketing FAST series, all available as Kindle Singles.

### Currently Available

1. The 4 Things You Must Know (to Make Money While You Sleep)
2. How to Select Your Internet Marketing Niche
3. How to Register a Domain Name
4. How to Host Your Website
5. WordPress for the Technically Challenged
6. Building Your Website with Thrive
7. The Thrive User
8. The Thrive Expert

### Yet to Be Written

9. Become an Affiliate Marketing Ninja
10. Become an E-Commerce Ninja
11. The Deadly Combo of Blog Posts and Landing Pages
12. Google is Your New Best Friend
13. Building Your Mailing List
14. All About Free and Paid Traffic
15. How to Publish Your Book on Amazon
16. The Secret to Making Money with Your Internet Businesses (after You've Done Everything Else)

The first eight books are available from Amazon in both Kindle and Paperback formats.

# How to Select Your IM Niche

A Fundamental Decision

## About the Author

As an 80 year old (in 2024) fitness fanatic and successful internet marketer, Phil Lancaster is a bit of an anomaly.

Through a combination of bad luck and bad business decisions, he found himself broke and alone at 74.

Now, some years later, he has several internet businesses that combine to bring him a 6-figure income.

It wasn't easy and he got burned a few times on the way, but he reckons that anyone can do it with the right road map.

He wants to help you to get started the way he did, but without making the same mistakes.

Anyone, from student to baby boomer (and older) can make money through the internet.

Phil's IM Fast series of mini-books will get you started. At just $2.99 each, you won't find a better investment.

www.ingramcontent.com/pod-product-compliance
Lightning Source LLC
Chambersburg PA
CBHW030547220526
45463CB00007B/3018